Delivering news to Monroe County for more than 105 years

No other product, endeavor, or activity connects a community quite the way a newspaper does. The Pocono Record has been the "bond" connecting area residents for more than 105 years.

The roots of the Pocono Record date back to 1894 with the publication of the *Stroudsburg Daily Times,* founded by George Hughes. This was Monroe County's first daily newspaper.

"Record" first appeared in the masthead as the *Monroe Record* in 1908, when the Monroe Publishing Company began production of a weekly paper. In 1920, Nelson Frantz bought the *Monroe Record* and combined it with the *Stroudsburg Daily Times.* The name *The Daily Record* was adopted.

Frantz sold the paper to Edward Breece near the end of World War II. On July 29, 1946, *The Daily Record* was purchased by Ottaway Newspapers, Inc., founded by Jim and Ruth Ottaway.

In 1965, the newspaper's name was changed to *The Pocono Record* to better reflect the area it served. Ottaway

Newspapers, Inc. joined Dow Jones & Company in 1970. In 1989, *"The"* was dropped from the masthead. The name *Pocono Record* remains today.

Historically, newspapers have kept an eye on government and institutions to uphold the First Amendment. The Pocono Record takes this responsibility seriously. We are the link for our growing communities, with local news, local issues, and local opinions.

Pocono Record
A reason to read... every day!

511 Lenox St., Stroudsburg – 570-421-3000
www.poconorecord.com

Monroe County
HISTORIC PHOTO ALBUM

PRESENTED BY THE POCONO RECORD & MONROE COUNTY HISTORICAL ASSOCIATION

TABLE OF CONTENTS

FOREWORD 4

TRANSPORTATION 5

STREET SCENES 17

COMMERCE 23

RESIDENTIAL 43

SCHOOLS & EDUCATION 53

SOCIETY 61

RECREATION & TOURISM 79

HERITAGE 105

VIEWS OF THE COUNTY 115

FEATURED BUSINESSES 119

FOREWORD

The photographs and postcards in this book focus on the first one hundred years of Monroe County, from 1836 until 1936. This joint project between the *Pocono Record* and the Monroe County Historical Association gives readers a glimpse of the rich heritage of our area.

From lumber rafts on the Delaware River to the elegant resorts in the mountains, the pictures reflect the many talents, interests, and enterprises of those who lived in Monroe County. Local citizens are featured as school children, merchants, athletes, factory workers and favorite relatives. Many area businesses, churches, scenes and buildings can still be recognized, even after a century of change.

The *Pocono Record* has been part of the Northeastern Pennsylvania community for more than 105 years. We're proud of our history, and we care about the future of this ever changing area. Throughout the past 105 years, we have remained true, continuing to provide news of importance and interest to the community. We're dedicated to being the number one information source for people and businesses of Monroe County.

The pictorial archives of the Monroe County Historical Association encompass a wide time span and show what life was like for the earlier settlers as well as the visitors who made this a prominent vacation area. MCHA has collected these archival reminders of the past since 1920 and continues to collect and preserve mementos of our past for future generations. We are delighted to be able to share our treasured resource with readers of this book.

Carolynn Allen-Evans
President and Publisher
Pocono Record

Candace McGreevy
Executive Director
Monroe County Historical Association

TRANSPORTATION

At first they came by stagecoach, wagon and on water. Then the railroad arrived in Monroe County in 1856, and a new era of transportation began, changing the landscape and opening opportunities.

The first train to come was from the Delaware, Lackawanna and Western line, traveling from Scranton to New York on May 13, 1856. The first depot was built that year, in Dansbury Manor, now called "East Stroudsburg" because of the railroad's identification. Soon the county was peppered with train stations.

Like the stage coach lines before it, the railroad led to creation of new villages and hospitality businesses. Moreover, it connected Monroe County with large urban centers, increasing market opportunities for such big Pocono crops as ice.

Tourism thrived as the increased comfort of travel brought more vacationers to the Poconos. The horse was still necessary for local transportation, however. Stagecoach routes laced the Poconos. Trolleys were pulled by mules, then by steam engines called dummies, and eventually by electricity.

Today, the only trolleys in existance are for sightseeing, and some of the old train depots have been turned into museums or a restaurant serving tourists who come by automobile. A high-speed train line is desired by commuters who travel from the Poconos to jobs in metropolitan areas. The existing railroad is used for hauling freight.

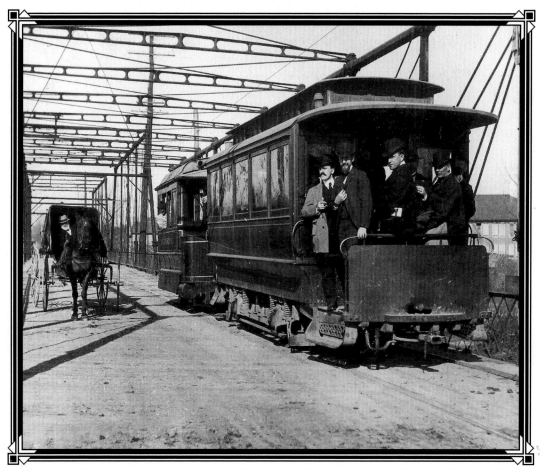

Trolley with dummy engine crossing the old State Bridge, now the Interboro Bridge, which connects Stroudsburg and East Stroudsburg. *#4656*

Passengers waiting for the train at Reeders Station. *#4996*

Delaware Valley Railroad Station, Bushkill.

New York, Susquehanna & Western Railroad freight station before it was moved to 537 Ann Street Stroudsburg, as the Driebe Freight Station.

Bartonsville Station before the railroad grade crossing. *#2286*

The Delaware, Lackawanna and Western train station along Crystal Street in East Stroudsburg, early 1900s.

Delaware House in Delaware Water Gap with the railroad station in the foreground, 1880s. *#3921*

Coming through the cut, Mount Pocono.

Lackawanna Railroad Station in Tobyhanna, circa 1915.

First engine rebuilt at Wilkes-Barre & Eastern Shops at Stroudsburg. It went into the shop March 15, 1894, and left May 8, 1894. J.W. Oplinger, foreman. *#3390*

Lackawanna Railway Station, Mount Pocono, circa 1905.

Delaware, Lackawanna and Western Station, Delaware Water Gap.

Water Gap Councilmen inspecting the new trolley line.

Tinkertown Crossing of the Delaware, Lackawanna & Western Railroad in Smithfield Township. #2288

Iron Bridge over the Creek connecting Stroudsburg and East Stroudsburg, circa 1905. This bridge was washed away by the flood of 1955.

Analomink Train wreck in 1910.

Two trolley cars running along Main Street in Stroudsburg. First trolley car (to the right) is for "Stroudsburg Passengers." The second is for "Analomink." *#4655*

Analomink wreck of the Delaware, Lackawanna & Western Railroad, 1910. *#3219*

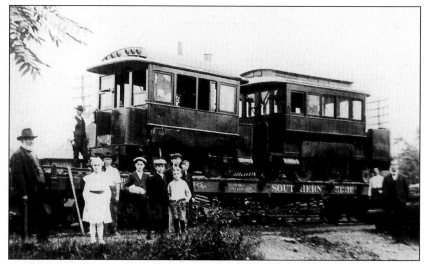

In 1895, engines called "dummies" pulled trolley cars. This trolley, on a flatbed, was headed to Stroudsburg where it would be unloaded. *#593*

Horsedrawn trolley with Ackerman's Flour Mill to the left, circa 1892. *#1701*

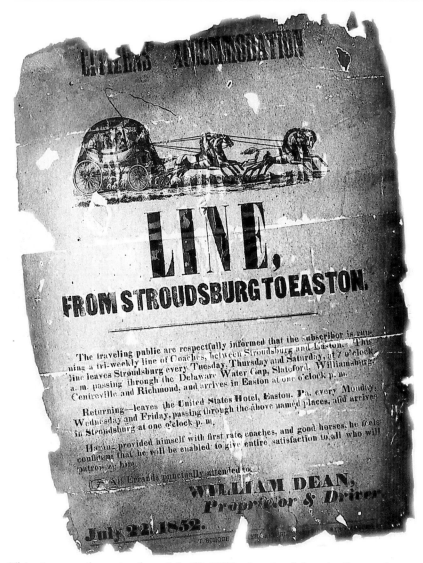

Covered bridge at Bartonsville, circa 1920.

Covered bridge at Bushkill. #517

This stagecoach poster from July 22, 1852 advertised that the line took passengers from the Stroudsburg to Easton three times a week. Travel time was six hours.

STREET SCENES

I t's hard to imagine, walking down busy Monroe County streets today, a time when they looked as broad and quiet as they do in these photos.

Streets were serious business in any town. One of the oldest responsibilities for a municipality is the maintenance of public thoroughfares. Most borough streets were not paved in the years before 1900, but attempts were made to keep them passable, and new equipment made their upkeep easier. Technological innovations such as electricity and new knowledge of sanitation contributed to new demands placed on municipal leaders. Meanwhile, residents were expected to help, too. In Stroudsburg, for instance, a law was passed by 1889 fining residents for throwing garbage in the streets instead of burning it in their yards.

Stroudsburg led Monroe County municipalities in street development because of its faster growth, but the more rural towns made the same improvements in time.

In 1889 Stroudsburg bought the county's first road machine, which was used to clean out gutters, level uneven areas and give the road a proper slope from the center to the gutters. Both Stroudsburg and East Stroudsburg hired the services of a street sprinkler to wet down dust on the roads. Lot

Main Street in Stroudsburg.

owners had to curb and pave sidewalks, the boroughs laid flagstone crossings to make it easier for pedestrians to cross muddy roads.

The first lamps, using burning oil, were put out in 1868 by Stroudsburg businessmen. By 1874, the borough was paying to have the

lamps lit each night although citizens were responsible for repairing the lamps, except for wicks and globes. Then electricity came along. Arc lights were put on Main Street in Stroudsburg in 1889 to stay lit until 2 a.m. every night except on bright moon-lit nights.

A view of lower Main Street, Stroudsburg after the flood of 1869. *#2230*

A panoramic view of Analomink, circa 1905.

Looking south down Race Street, Kresgeville.

Thomas Street in Stroudsburg, circa 1907.

Church Street in Tobyhanna, circa 1910.

Scott Street in Stroudsburg.

Willow Dell, North Water Gap.

Main Street in McMichaels.

Washington Street, East Stroudsburg, circa 1910. *#5068*

The Old Pines and Bridge, Canadensis.

State Road through Marshalls Creek.

Among the cottages at Mount Pocono.

Main Street,
Brodheadsville,
circa 1910.

Main Street in
Brodheadsville, show-
ing the post office and
general store.

COMMERCE

Lumber and agriculture in the summer, ice in the winter, tourists year-round to enjoy the beauty - from natural resources grew Monroe County's first industries.

Sawmills turned timber into lumber. Bark suitable for tanning hides prompted tannery construction in Barrett Township, Stroudsburg and other sites. Grist mills ground agricultural crops.

Bricks were made from Kunkleton to East Stroudsburg. Evergreens became Christmas trees and holiday decorations, while elsewhere on the mountain, huckleberries, chestnuts, hickory nuts, and maple syrup were harvested. Quarrying operations yielded flagstone, building stone, slate and sand. Ice houses on Saylor's Lake, Trout Lake, Mountain Spring Lake, Lake Naomi, Stillwater Lake, Pocono Lake and lakes at Tobyhanna thrived until electricity made the need to refrigerate with ice obsolete. Water from Ross Commons Springs, long appreciated for its curative properties, was being bottled by 1888 for sale throughout the East.

With the Industrial Revolution, manufacturing began in earnest in the late 1900s, and Monroe County companies put the area's healthy wood supply to use in making clothespins, shoe pegs, window sashes, brooms, matches, barrel hoops, baskets, pulp and paper, piano stools and other needs. Waste leather scraps from tanning were combined with tanite to make solid emery wheels.

Fred Scheller Fancy Grocery Store, 8th and Main Street, Stroudsburg. *#1063*

Mills and factories prompted development of other businesses to repair and service their iron tools and machinery. As the population grew, so did the need for retail shops and shopping districts to supply goods ranging from foods to clothing to gift items for tourists. Shopping districts thrived in Stroudsburg, East Stroudsburg and other areas with large varieties to offer consumers. Retailing innovations included the chain store, and in 1911 Stroudsburg became the site of the first of J.J. Newberry's nationwide chain of "5 and 10 cent stores."

Wirt T. Miller Grocery Store at 720 Main Street in Stroudsburg, circa 1910. Included in the picture are Mr. Miller, Herbert Heller and Stewart Swartwood.

Witte's Fish Market, 13 South 7th Street, Stroudsburg. John and Mary Witte are waiting for customers in 1924. #3889

H. G. Rhodes Butcher shop was at 517 Main Street in Stroudsburg. This delivery wagon was used in 1913. #5144

Kohl's Bakery was located on West Main Street in Stroudsburg. The bakery wagon made deliveries about 1920. #3497

Pipher's Bakery, as early as 1913, had a large wholesale business in and around the county. The bakery was between Sarah Street and Quaker Alley in Stroudsburg. *#3157*

The annual Wyckoff Department Store party was held at Mount Vernon, VA, on February 22, 1929. The Wyckoff Band was part of the festivities. *#3527*

Wallace's Department Store about 1910. It was on Main Street in Stroudsburg.

Store in Reeders with a delivery wagon in the front. *#4995*

Shawnee Store, circa 1908.

Tobyhanna Store, established in 1862.

Alleger's Store, Bartonsville.

Saylorsburg Ice Company. #455

Seguine and Shannon was called "The Cresco Cash Store" when it opened in 1891. #836

Lakes and ponds provided ice for many cities on the East Coast. This was an offshoot of the lumber industry when the splash dams froze in the winter. #999

The seaming department of the Mammoth Hosiery Mill on Main Street in Stroudsburg. #3615

Mountain Spring Ice Plant, Reeders. #14

Brown & Keller began in 1910, near the Interboro Bridge in East Stroudsburg, to make furniture and furnishings for home and business use. They were also the local undertakers. *#1818*

Grist Mill, 7th and Main, Stroudsburg. LaBar's Harness shop is on the right. In 1840, Monroe County had 25 grist mills, 10 saw mills and a population of 1879. *#5110*

Col. John VanCampen operated a grist mill at Shawnee in 1758 and shipped flour via Durham boats to Philadelphia. Vestiges of the old mill are still visible. *#2704*

Millstone found in McMichaels Creek in Stroudsburg from a very early mill. It is currently at the Stroud Mansion. *#527*

Shawnee Mill built in 1753 made electric power for Charles C. Worthington, builder of Shawnee Inn. Circa, 1905. *#413*

Foundation of the oldest flour mill in Paradise Township, 1849. *#3477*

Old paper mill about 1900. The timber industry was a mainstay of the Monroe County economy. *#1371*

Analomink Sawmill owned by C.A. Coleman, circa 1926. *#1605*

Invitation for the lamb dinner held on May 18, 1898. Thomas Kitson and the Kitson Woolen Mills set a new world's record, "From Sheep to Suit" in six hours and four minutes.

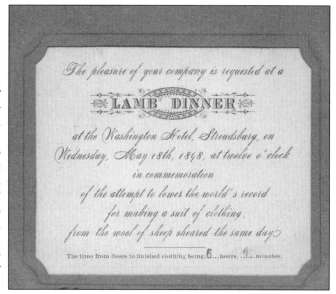

Pipher's Mill and Silver Lake Falls, North Water Gap.

Kitson Woolen Mill in Stroudsburg.

Kunkle's Mill, Kresgeville.

Eilenberger's Mill, North Water Gap, circa 1905.

The Hollinshead Drug Store shown in 1865 was located on Main Street near 7th Street in Stroudsburg. The first building on the left was the office of Dr. Jackson. The carriage on the right is in front of Judge Dreher's office. *#3066*

Fawn Cabin Restaurant, Echo Lake.

The Yin Hoo Cha Yuan Silver Lake Tea House was built in 1924 by Mrs. Ernest Hogg. She modeled her tea room in Minisink Hills after the Empress DoWager's summer palace in China.

Shoemaker in Bartonsville, circa 1904.

The Times and Democrat was published between 1907 and 1917. This building was on Main near 6th Street in Stroudsburg.

The Piano Stool Factory in East Stroudsburg, circa 1914. *#5173*

East Stroudsburg Glass Works employees in 1893. They began production in 1877 and reached 35,000 gross of bottles annually. *#2648*

Stroudsburg Cut Glass Company, Scott Street, Stroudsburg, 1915. *#3837*

Bell Telephone workers installing lines in Cresco, circa 1912. *#3235*

Glass or spectacles factory in Cherry Valley. Rollo LaBar is standing on the right in the doorway. *#3640*

Tag day workers for General Hospital (now Pocono Medical Center) taken on the lawn of Mrs. J.W. Booth, July 9, 1920. Her home was on the corner of Analomink Street and Ransberry Avenue in East Stroudsburg. *#1758*

R. H. Kintner and Co. coal yard at 312 Main Street in Stroudsburg, circa 1913. *#08*

Kautz Stables and Wagon Shop, Stroudsburg.

The Holland Manufacturing Company made silk thread at the plant on Lower Main Street, Stroudsburg. *#835*

John Gardner at his blacksmith shop in Delaware Water Gap, circa 1910. *#375*

A local blacksmith at work in 1918. *#1559*

The Blue Ridge Enamel Brick Company was located in Saylorsburg, where there was a good vein of clay. Incorporated in April 1894 as the Penn Buff Brick and Tile Company, the factory at first produced only front brick. Realizing the market for enameled brick, the company started production in the fall of 1898 of "high-grade, hard-glaze, mud-made, enameled brick." The name was changed in April 1901. A large operation, Blue Ridge Brick, owned several structures as well as 200 to 300 acres of land used for digging clay. The company also owned the Lake House at Saylorsburg. In 1901, 150 men and boys were employed at the plant. *#528*

Logging scene by McMichaels photographer Professor Philip Kishpaugh. *#1101*

Jacob Kintz, a jobber of cigars for wholesale and retail. The store was located on Main Street, Stroudsburg, 1900. *#2805*

Swiftwater Labs established as Slee Laboratories in 1897, now Aventis Pasteur, manufacturer of vaccines, circa 1933. *#2064*

Fred Eilenberger, Clinton Staples, Dr. J.H. Shull and Clinton Eilenberger are ready to send the log raft down the river. Rafting continued until 1910. #917

RESIDENTIAL

Just as a picture is worth 1,000 words, residential architecture tells a story of Monroe County's development, from the old stone houses in Shawnee-on-Delaware and Sciota where early settlers lived, to the ornate Victorian residences of the Stroudburgs. Many of those pictured here still exist, albeit changed to suit the needs of their various occupants over the years.

On Main Street in Stroudsburg, many of the elegant old houses are now occupied by attorneys offices, businesses and non-profit organizations. The Stroud Mansion, built by Jacob Stroud in 1795 for his son, Daniel, escaped destruction in 1920 when the Civic Club of Stroudsburg intervened. The home remains a local landmark as it is now a museum.

Houses along Sarah, Scott and Thomas streets are like mansions, with architecture ranging from Gothic to Victorian to Colonial. The stately residence shown on this page of A. Mitchell Palmer, a U.S. Attorney General under President Woodrow Wilson and an unsuccessful presidential candidate, still stands, peeking out from behind a tall wall of shrubs and trees on Thomas Street. On Broad Street, the gracious old Kintner home (page 48) is now a professional building.

In East Stroudsburg, head west on Washington Street and you'll spot the dwelling (page 46) of Hannah Stroud Starbird. It's changed

A. Mitchell Palmer residence on Thomas Street in Stroudsburg.

over the past two centuries, with a large addition and dormers among other modifications.

To the southwest, you'll still find Linden Court in Sciota at the intersection of Route 209 and Business Route 209. In Sciota, the Fenner/Snyder/Robacker homestead, built in 1805, belongs to Hamilton Township now and is open periodically for tours. Some of the rooms contain period furnishings. Across the street from it is the old Sciota Mill, purportedly used by Gen. Sullivan's troops during his march against the Iroquois.

The Joseph Jefferson Cottage was located in Paradise Valley. It contained 12 to 15 rooms. Joseph Jefferson was a famous actor in the 1850s who depicted many popular characters including Rip Van Winkle.

The first telephone line connected in Monroe County in 1893 ran 13 miles from the Peter's House in Bushkill to the Delaware Lackawanna, and Western Railroad Station on Crystal Street in East Stroudsburg.

The Stroud Mansion house on the corner of 9th and Main Streets in Stroudsburg was built in 1795 by Jacob Stroud. In 1920, the Civic Club of Stroudsburg saved the house from destruction and in 1994 the Woman's Club of the Stroudsburgs transferred ownership to the Monroe County Historical Association.

Linden Court was a charming resort and restaurant located in Sciota.

Mansion House, Kresgeville.

The Gonsalez family members were early settlers who lived along the Delaware River in Middle Smithfield Township.

Christian Kautz home on River Road north of Shawnee, circa 1900. Included in the photo, left to right, Mrs. Sarah (Clark) Kautz, Miss Bertha Kautz, unidentified, Miss Laura Koher and Christian Kautz. *#0212*

Peter Eilenberger home in Shawnee, circa 1901. *#0213*

Dwelling of Hannah (Stroud) Starbird on Washington Street in East Stroudsburg (October 11, 1763 - December 14, 1839). Hannah was the daughter of Jacob and Elizabeth (McDowell) Stroud. *#0027*

Stroud Mansion in the 1920s. *#2803*

Residences on Main Street, Stroudsburg. *#101*

Home of Simon Meixell, circa late 1800s. Included in the photo are, left to right, John U. Meixell, Simon Meixell (builder, owner), Lizzie Keller Meixell with baby, Harold K Meixell, Mabel Meixell and Sophia Cornellia Metzgar Meixell. *#0433*

Home of Deborah (Stroud) Burson (January 25, 1782 - August 4, 1866) built by Deborah's father, Jacob Stroud. The house was located in East Stroudsburg *#5109*

The Kintner home on Broad Street in Stroudsburg. *#102*

Home at 6th and Main Streets in Stroudsburg. *#1070*

Two ladies standing on Dearr Street with their backs to the Sam Scott house at 152 N. Courtland in East Stroudsburg, circa 1912. *#3498*

Interior of Leila Beers home at 604 Sarah Street in Stroudsburg. *#0896*

House at 239 S. Courtland Street in East Stroudsburg where the Civil Liberties Union parking lot now stands. *#0877*

Polly Counterman in the doorway of her house on Smokey Hill Road.

An early years duplex. On the left is the Carmer family home. On the right is the Palmer family home. *#4967*

Scotrun new two-room building, dedicated February 13, 1915. *#5126*

Dr. David C. Trach's (1891-1937) residence in Kresgeville. *#3525*

Home of Robert Reading Depuy in Shawnee. *#1725*

Home at 601 Thomas Street in Stroudsburg prior to 1925. *#4865*

The Fenner/Snyder/Robacker homestead in Sciota was built in 1805 by Barnett Fenner. The stone farmhouse now belongs to Hamilton Township.

SCHOOLS & EDUCATION

The earliest school anyone could remember in Monroe County was on Keever's Hill in Stroud Township, County Superintendent of Schools B.F. Morey reported in 1876. It was organized sometime before 1800 by Daniel Stroud, John Stroud, Mr. Hollinshead and others, and was later moved to Stroudsburg adjacent to the Friends' meeting house. The first teacher was a Mr. Curtis.

At Hamilton Square in Hamilton Township, a log structure, like the one in Stroudsburg, operated at about the same time. In Middle Smithfield, a school was organized by the Coolbaughs and Overfields in an old log dwelling. The first school house built in Chestnuthill Township was in a double house, with the German-born teacher and his family living on one half, and school in the other. In 1816, the first school in Pocono Township was organized in a spring house in Tannersville.

In the western part of the county, schools were taught entirely in German or, at best, in German and English. They were entirely supported by subscription.

The first schools essentially were one-room school houses operated largely by teachers with little or no formal training. That was changing by 1900.

The East Stroudsburg State Normal School opened on Sept. 4, 1893, with 320 pupils. Many of the first graduates were employed in Monroe

Faculty of East Stroudsburg Normal School, now East Stroudsburg University of Pennsylvania, 1901. *#68*

County Schools. Prior to then, only seven "Normal" graduates were teaching in the county. By 1900, there were 46, nearly all from the East Stroudsburg school.

The Normal School was the third institution of higher education in Monroe County. At the West End, the county had two academies: Fairview, founded in 1881, and the Polytechnic Institute in 1886 in Gilbert. They, too, contributed to the teacher pool, with Fairview providing 47 and Polytechnic, 19 of the 151 teachers in Monroe County in 1900.

Students on steps of East Stroudsburg State Normal School. *#3593*

East Stroudsburg Normal School in 1895. This was the original Stroud Hall, called "Old Main." *#2586*

Fairview Academy was built in 1881 in Brodheadsville and was active until 1938.

Public School and M.E. Church, Analomink, circa 1906.

Shafer's Schoolhouse was built in 1823. For 30 years, it was also used as a church by English and German Lutherans. It was discontinued as a school in the early 1900s. *#3111*

Interior view of Bell School which is now the property of the Monroe County Historical Association. *#901*

Barrett High School, Canadensis, circa 1912.

Bell School, a one-room schoolhouse along Cherry Valley Road was built in the 1870s and housed students until 1953. *#3141*

Miss Lillie Bittenbender's first-grade class in 1892. Miss Lillie was a favorite Stroudsburg teacher for over 48 years. It was estimated that she taught over thirty-five hundred students.

Eilenberger's (Hollow) one room school from 1901, located at Shawnee-on-Delaware. *#1030*

Central High School in Gilbert, Polk Township. Photo was taken December 7, 1909. *#2694*

Dr. Mary Grenwald Erdman's (seated left) medical class of 1872 at Blockly Hospital, now Pennsylvania General Hospital. *#2736*

East Stroudsburg Public School, first grade, 1892. *#1027*

East Stroudsburg High School seniors at Mount Vernon, Virginia, 1930. *#5257*

Graduating
class of 1925,
Stroudsburg
High School.
The school
burned down
two years later.

#3622

Fire at Stroudsburg High School which was located at 6th and Thomas streets. School burned February 26, 1927, and was destroyed. Ramsey School now stands on the property. *#3473*

Stroudsburg High School, class of 1896. *#556*

Stroudsburg High School, class of 1926. *#3923*

East Stroudsburg State Normal School orchestra, 1893-1900. *#5112*

Rear of Stroudsburg High School, from Crowley's Hill. The front of the school is on Thomas Street, Stroudsburg. Before 1905. *#5069*

SOCIETY

When there's a need, there's a person or a group in Monroe County who can fill it, it seems.

High schools many years ago listed as a priority "the worthy use of leisure time." For many, that translates into membership in a myriad of social and civic organizations that have assisted the needy, changed politics, built medical facilities and churches, bettered our schools, preserved our history, helped our children, entertained us with music and arts and generally improved our communities.

Their purposes often overlapped. During World War II, for instance, Red Cross and the Stroudsburg Woman's Club worked together to present nutritional programs at the YMCA. Volunteer emergency medical aides were trained at the C.L.U. club in East Stroudsburg. The Kiwanis salvaged rubber and scrap iron and promoted Victory Gardens to help with rationing efforts.

The Monroe County Hospital was started in 1906 by eight men in the George Heller Home on Sarah Street in Stroudsburg. The General Hospital was started in 1915 on North Courtland Street in a location now occupied by the East Stroudsburg United Methodist Church. It moved to the present site of Pocono Medical Center on East Brown Street and in 1930 merged with the Monroe County Hospital. Many of its facilities have been financed over the years through donations and charitable work.

Monroe Delegation, circa 1900. *#1417*

Civic pride drew volunteers to fight fires or to dedicate careers to emergency services, police work or other vital services such as rounding up horse thieves. The Phoenix Fire Engine and Hose Company #2 of Stroudsburg was the first, formed in September 26, 1845. Likewise, the military appealed to the loyalties of Monroe County residents who have fought for their country since the Revolutionary War. They've helped in other ways, too; vaccines produced by Dr. Richard Slee in Swiftwater – at what is now Aventis Pasteur – were shipped to Cuba in 1898 to assist soldiers who stricken by disease in the Spanish American War.

Ticket to the first Annual Ball of G.M. Wallace Lodge, No. 382, Brotherhood of Railroad Trainmen at Odd fellows Hall on April 22, 1891. #523

Keystone Band, Pocono Lake. #83.156.01

Worthington Hall in Shawnee, circa 1906.

C. B. Huff in his band uniform.

Rockefeller Band, circa 1912.

Wyckoff's Boy's Band, sponsored by Wyckoff's Department Store, May 1933. *#3865*

Stroudsburg Band at the Clambake for the employees of International Boiler Works and Patterson Kelly Co. at the Lutheran Ministerium Camp, circa 1924. *#0210*

A noted American harp soloist, Ethel Dean West played the harp for many leading orchestras including the NBC Symphony of the Air and the New York Philharmonic. #2307

In June 1931, the Poconos celebrated the first Laurel Blossom Time Festival to honor Pennsylvania's state flower. These young ladies were the Laurel Princesses and were guests of the Kittatinny Hotel in Delaware Water Gap, 1931. #1424

Howard Arndt standing in Matangas, Cuba, during the Spanish American War, February 2, 1901. #2A.216.03

Wedding processional in Swiftwater. The bride is in the first horse-drawn carriage. #3402

A group of soldiers celebrates winning a shooting trophy. Earl Kresge is the third from right. *#4123*

Teddy Roosevelt visiting the Water Gap House, Delaware Water Gap, circa 1910.

Courthouse staff in front of the courthouse, January 4, 1932. *#4188*

Portrait of A. Mitchell Palmer (1872-1936). A Quaker, he was U.S. Attorney General under President Woodrow Wilson from 1919 to 1921. He declared himself a presidential candidate in 1920, but did not receive nomination. He later practiced law in Stroudsburg. *#1780*

East Stroudsburg Volunteer Fire Company, circa 1915. *#4555*

Theodore H. Welter (1855-1927) served as the chief of police of Stroudsburg for over 38 years. His brother, Abraham V. Welter, was chief of police in East Stroudsburg at the same time.

Pocono No. 1, 1871 Clapp and Jones steam fire engine. Known as "der mercheen." Owned by the Phoenix Fire Engine and Hose Company, No. 2, Stroudsburg. *#3379*

Acme Hose Company, East Stroudsburg Fire Department. *#5122*

Knights of Malta Parade by the East Stroudsburg Railroad Station, on Crystal Street, circa 1915. *#4197*

Octogenarian Club in front of Stuart Shafer's home at 801 Main Street, October 10, 1913. *#67*

Methodist Church in Swiftwater, established in 1855.

Located in Bartonsville, the St. John's Evangelical Congregation Church was built in 1892.

The Zion Union Church was built in the Gravel Hill's section of Brodheadsville in 1862.

Interior of Hamilton Square Church. *#2724*

McComas Chapel in Price Township was erected in 1867. *#2079*

Church of St. Ann, Canadensis, circa 1912.

Library in the Stroud Community House, Stroudsburg.

East Stroudsburg Methodist Church Men's Brotherhood, 1915. *#5168*

The Monroe County Horse Brigade was an organization which took the place of the State Police. Members rounded up horse thieves and returned stolen horses to their owners. This picture was taken at their annual banquet at the Indian Queen Hotel in Stroudsburg in 1884. *#3205*

Flora Snyder Kautz, wife of John J. Kautz, Stroudsburg, circa 1888. *#2798*

George LaBar, 1733-1838, oldest man in Monroe County lived to be 105 years old. *#4059*

Samboe's Creek flows through East Stroudsburg. *#138*

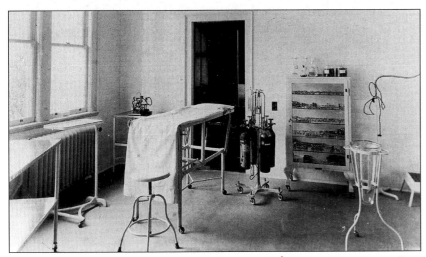

Operating room at The General Hospital at 206 East Brown Street, East Stroudsburg, circa 1923. *#2202*

Pohoqualine Fish Association Club House, McMichaels, which began in 1894.

Florence Smith (left), about 6 years old, and Laura B. Smith, 8 years old, were sisters who lived in Stroudsburg. *#4871 & #4870*

Ladies Aid of North Water Gap taken at Aaron Fowler's home, 1913. *#429*

Fourth Liberty Loan Headquarters. In the photo are: Mrs. Edith Brown, Mrs. Sally Booth, unknown woman, Rev. Emmons, Mrs. C.B. Staples, Harry Albert, Louise Congdon, Mrs. Gilbert. #66

RECREATION & TOURISM

The Pocono region has long been a playground for visitors, celebrities and dignitaries drawn by the spectacular Delaware Water Gap and beauty of the surrounding mountains and woodlands.

A ferry and wagon road transported visitors along the Delaware River to the Delaware Water Gap - listed as one of the country's 15 scenic marvels in 1910 when President Theodore Roosevelt visited. The Water Gap's attraction to musicians and artists drew such famous entertainers as John Philip Sousa, Fanny Brice and Enrico Caruso. In Paradise Township, Roosevelt and Presidents Grover Cleveland, Benjamin Harrison and Calvin Coolidge stayed at the Henryville House Fishing Hotel, which also hosted such celebrities as Buffalo Bill Cody.

Hotels, motels, lodges, campgrounds, taverns, restaurants and resorts are as abundant as the waterfalls, wooded hills, festivals and recreation facilities that lure visitors. One of the first to lodge tourists was the famous Kittatiny Hotel in Delaware Water Gap, initially constructed in 1829 and destroyed by fire 102 years later. The now-defunct Inn at Buck Hill opened the Poconos' first golf course in 1904 and introduced the region to such winter sports as skiing and tobogganing. Skytop is famous for its five-story-high resort with fantastic views and a reputation in its early years for such novel activities as ice skating while being pulled by a tractor or skiing

Wyckoff's Boys Club band, circa 1930. *#3887*

with aid from an airplane.

In the mid 1870s, the railroad led to development of the Mount Pocono area as a resort region treasured for its views and outdoor recreation.

The first state park was located at Snow Hill in Price Township and was an outgrowth of a Civilian Conservation Corps Camp during the Great Depression of the 1930s. Today, there are many parks, state game lands and lakes that are favorites for hunters, anglers, hikers and campers. The world-famous Appalachian Trail now brings travelers by foot, as they stop in Monroe County for a rest and supplies while hiking from Maine to Georgia.

Boatlanding at Delaware Water Gap, circa 1900.

The Champion in the Field Day Sports, Tobyhanna, circa 1914.

Caldeno golf links, Delaware Water Gap.

A man on a canoe on the Delaware River near Buckwood Inn (now Shawnee Inn), 1922. *#1659*

McMichaels Creek Biesecker's Camp, August, 1903. *#634*

Monroe Countians gathered at the fairgrounds.

Stroudsburg Fair Grounds located where the present Stroudsburg High School was built in 1979. #3328

Patterson Kelly picnic, Saylorsburg Lake, August 20, 1927. #4106

Young people by the river, circa 1912.

Trout Ponds, McMichaels.

Moonlight on the Delaware, Delaware Water Gap, circa 1910.

Clam bake. *#3862*

Doll party, January 14, 1926. *#3866*

Fred Waring's Pennsylvanians recording the "Old Gold Hour," 1933. *#3579*

Indian Queen Hotel, Main Street, Stroudsburg. *#0461*

Ready for a mountain climb, Delaware Water Gap, circa 1903.

The Dam, Bartonsville, circa 1908.

Storytelling around the campfire, 1930. *#3243*

Brookside Farm in Henryville. *#3262*

Height 10 feet; weight when killed, near half ton. Mounted for B. P. O. E. Lodge No. 319. This Elk represents our Secret Process of

TANNING BEFORE MOUNTING

which we now use in all our work.

THE GUARANTEE TAXIDERMIST
STROUDSBURG, PENNA.
BOTH PHONES   (over)

An early taxidermy advertisement.

Pohoqualine baseball team, 1908. *#1636*

Stroudsburg High School football team, 1928. *#2718*

East Stroudsburg High School basketball team, 1927-1928. *#3229*

Castle Inn Music Hall, Delaware Water Gap.

Churleigh Inn Park, Stroudsburg.

Rolling Hills Lodge in Paradise Valley, Cresco.

East Porch, Buck Hill Inn.

East Room fireplace, Buck Hill Inn.

Smoking room at Buck Hill Inn.

Indian Queen Hotel on Main Street in Stroudsburg, circa 1910. The first automobile in the Poconos stopped here in August 1899.

Banker's Banquet at the Indian Queen Hotel, January 27, 1912, given by President Charles Dean Wallace for the Directors and Officials of the Stroudsburg National Bank. *#2242*

Washington House on the corner of 5th and Main in Stroudsburg.

The Buckwood Inn (now Shawnee Inn) swimming pool and paddling pool in Shawnee-on-Delaware, built in 1906.

Hotel Fulmer in Stroudsburg at 7th and Main Streets. Now Best Western Pocono Inn.

Forest Inn, Bartonsville.

Rebuilding of the Kittatinny Hotel in Delaware Water Gap. It was built in 1829, renovated twice and rebuilt in 1884. It had accommodations for 275 guests before it burned to the ground in 1931. *#1429*

Kittatinny Hotel in Delaware Water Gap. *#2223*

Kittatinny Hotel, view from the veranda. *#84.28.7*

Interior of the Kittatinny Hotel. *#676c*

Spruce Cabin Inn, Canadensis, circa 1920.

Spruce Cabin Inn, Canadensis, circa 1910.

The Lodge at Skytop Club located three miles north of Canadensis. Skytop Lodge has been serving visitors and tourists in the Pocono Mountains since 1928.

The Naomi Pines House, Pocono Pines.

Laurel Inn Dining Room, Pocono Lake, circa 1915.

Laurel Inn, Pocono Lake, circa 1915.

Lake House, Saylorsburg, circa 1902.

Lutherland in Pocono Pines drew campers and vacationers from 2,000 Lutheran congregations.

Water Gap House in Delaware Water Gap.

Brodheads Cottage, Delaware Water Gap.

The Dutot Museum is the former schoolhouse in Delaware Water Gap, which was called Dutotsburg.

Forest Inn, Bartonsville.

Turn Villa, 12 miles from Stroudsburg.

Exchange and office of the Ontwood Hotel, Mt. Pocono.

Hilldrup Summer Home, Analomink, circa 1914.

Parkside House in Henryville. Parkside was an early name of Henryville. *#1517*

Harrison Park, Blakeslee.

Penn Stroud Hotel, once the Stroudsburg House kept by Stroud Hollinshead. Now the Best Western Pocono Inn at 7th and Main Streets in Stroudsburg. *#884*

Fernest Cottage in Shawnee-on-Delaware, near the entrance to the Buckwood Inn, 1922. *#1052*

The "Giant's Foot" was carved out by the Cherry Creek in Cherry Valley, circa 1900. *#2121*

The American Hotel in the center of Kunkletown is said to have been opened by Joseph Kunkle in 1849. *#3367*

American House, 8th and Main Streets in Stroudsburg. *#885a*

The Glenwood House, a non-sectarian academy from 1855-1862, was said to be the best school building built in Monroe County. As Delaware Water Gap became a popular tourist destination, the school closed and the Glenwood House opened for guests. *#865*

Manwalamink in Shawnee-on-Delaware. Before elaborate additions it was Fort Dupuy, a frontier fort. *#1365*

Cliff View Cottage in Cresco could accommodate 50 guests, about 1/2 mile from the Cresco Station. The original building was a stagecoach stop as early as 1813. *#12*

HERITAGE

Monroe County's landscape, like its history, is sprinkled liberally with names like Stroud, Brodhead, Kresge and Depui. Some helped create a new country while creating new settlements here. Jacob Stroud, for example, was an officer in the Revolutionary Army and founded Stroudsburg. Nicholas Depui and Manuel Gonsalez, from Smithfield Township, were members of Committees of Observation that supervised the boycott of British goods.

Kresgeville is named for the Kresge family, whose members over the years have included chain store magnate S.S. Kresge, who donated $25,000 in 1928 to the school district. Daniel Brodhead was an early settler of what is now East Stroudsburg, and his name lives on in local geography through the Brodhead Creek, Dansbury Park and more.

Dutch and German settlers were first in the area. They and other early settlers came from cultures in which the Protestant Christian Church was important, and they brought their beliefs here as evidenced in the variety of churches - German Reformed, Lutheran Reformed, Methodist, Presbyterian, German Evangelical and more. One of the first churches was erected in 1753 in Shawnee and, over the years, was led by Dutch Reformed, Lutheran and Presbyterian pastors. Its foundations were used for the present Shawnee Presbyterian Church. The Great Awakening, which was sweeping American religious life, is seen in

Eight Brodhead Brothers were descendants of General Daniel Brodhead, early settler in East Stroudsburg, originally called Dansbury. *#3138*

camp meetings that were popular in Monroe County during the 1840s and 1850s.

Along Highways 940 and 611, you'll see historical markers for the Sullivan Trail, which is the path used by Gen. John Sullivan and his troops on their northward march against the Iroquois Indians in 1779. Others from the area who have achieved national attention include A. Mitchell Palmer, a Quaker who served as United States attorney general under President Woodrow Wilson and later ran unsuccessfully for president, and John Summerfield Staples, a Stroudsburg native who was President Abraham Lincoln's representative recruit in the federal army during the Civil War.

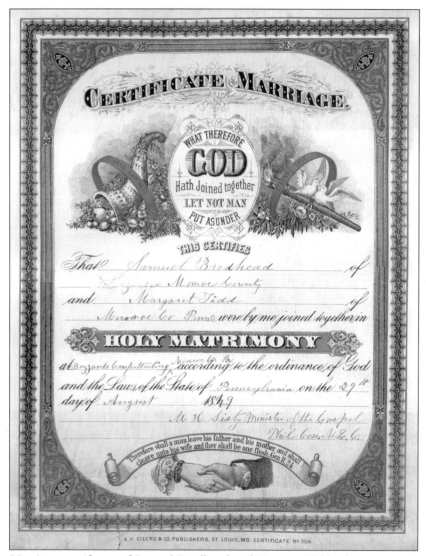

Marriage certificate of Samuel Brodhead and Margaret Tidd who were married August 29, 1849.

Luke W. Brodhead, a famous local historian (1821-1902). #3830

Samuel Brodhead (1826-1907).

Margaret Tidd Brodhead (1830-1905).

Site of Fort Penn and early home of Jacob Stroud, founder of Stroudsburg. *#3888*

Monroe County Courthouse, built in 1839 by Monroe County's first commissioners; Henry Fenner, Joseph Trach, and Jacob Shoemaker. It once stood on the corner of 7th and Monroe Streets, near where the modern Courthouse stands today. *#1419*

Portrait of Daniel Stroud (1772-1846), son of Stroudsburg's founder, Jacob Stroud. Daniel was a lawyer in Easton, but moved up to the Stroud Mansion to assist his father in developing Stroudsburg and the surrounding area.

Photo by Ken Schurman.

Members of Monroe County Historical Society, circa 1936. Left to right: Dr. Mary Erdman, President, Dr. Robert Brown, Secretary, Carl Clausson, Jacob Knauf, Mrs. N.A. Frantz, Dr. Robert Brown Keller, Dr. Nathan Meyer. *#422*

The dedication of cannons at Courthouse Square, Stroudsburg, circa 1890.

Methodist revival meeting in Delaware Water Gap, circa 1900. As camp meetings' popularity grew, open fields became places to sponsor and house these revival gatherings. *#3839*

The Beakleyville Baptist Church was established in the summer of 1843. A series of revival meetings conducted by Rev. Joseph Currin, a Baptist missionary, resulted in 43 converts to the Baptist faith. This church was built at Eagle Valley Corners in East Stroudsburg to house the new congregation. *#157D*

The Presbyterian Church of the Mountain in Delaware Water Gap was organized in 1854. It was established to serve not only the residents, but also the tourists who visited the area. *#3551*

The Christ Church in Hamilton Township was organized in 1768. Both the Lutheran and Reformed congregations met there. *#59A*

Foundation of the Shawnee Presbyterian Church. Headstones from the earlier church are part of the foundations for new one. Original church dates from 1752. *#2917*

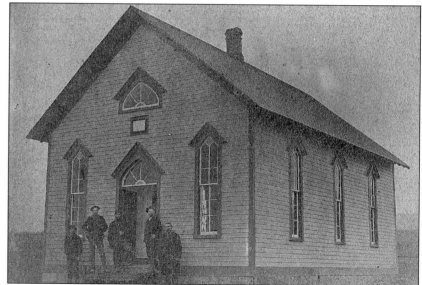

The Reeders Methodist Church was built in 1883 and was part of the Tannersville Circuit. This church shared one minister with three other churches. Pictured, left to right: Ed Possinger, Theodore Woodling, Jacob Doll, Mike Woodling, and the Rev. G.W. Dugan, who dedicated the church. *#3621*

Photo of Mt. Zion Methodist Church on Chipperfield Drive in Stroudsburg. It once housed the Holy Trinity Eastern Orthodox Church and is now privately owned. *#174*

The Shawnee Presbyterian Church replaced the "Old Stone Church" which was erected in 1752 and used by various Christian denominations, including Presbyterians, Lutherans, Baptists, and German and Dutch Reformed. *#2629*

Although the Cherry Valley Methodist Church was not built until 1843, Methodist prayer meetings had been held as early as 1830.

Located in the Salem Union Church Cemetery in Gilbert, the Kresge monument depicts the violence between early settlers and Native Americans. Conrad Kresge's 12-year old son, John, was killed by Indians in 1757. *#84*

Headstone of Phillip Bossert. #647

Headstone of Elizabeth Siglie who was born August 15, 1773 and died August 4, 1811. Monroe County was home to many settlers from Germany as noted by her headstone. #852

Believed to be an Indian trail marker located on the John Kresge farm in Kresgeville. #894B

Hollinshead Cemetery located on Dreher Avenue, Stroudsburg. Stroud J. Hollinshead was the grandson of Jacob Stroud. He built the Stroudsburg House in 1833, now the Best Western on Main Street.

Brinker's Mill, or the Old Mill at Sciota, was believed to be a resting place for General John Sullivan and his troops in 1779 on their march northward against the Iroquois Indians.

A family photo of the Arnold children taken in Stroudsburg about 1886. Left to right: Goldie Arnold, Nellie Arnold and Arthur E. Arnold.

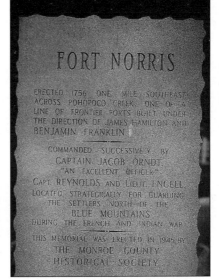

Historical marker for Fort Norris, which was located one mile south of Route 209 near Kresgeville. This fort was commissioned by Benjamin Franklin to protect early settlers in the area from Indians. #203

General John Sullivan and his troops camped at Hungry Hill in 1779. The militia had been sent northward by General George Washington to defend the area against Iroquois Indians. This memorial marks the resting place of an unknown Revolutionary War Soldier. #888

John Summerfield Staples, a private in the Union Army served in the 2nd Regiment of District of Columbia Volunteers for nearly a year before returning to Stroudsburg. He was also the representative recruit for President Abraham Lincoln. *#2106*

The volunteer enlistment of John Summerfield Staples. *#2107*

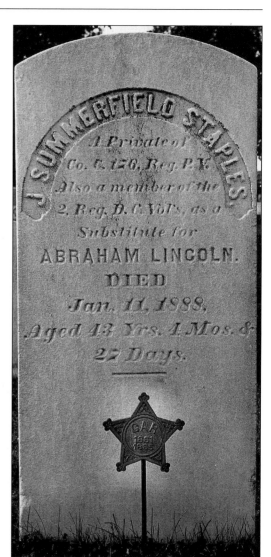

Headstone of John Summerfield Staples found in Stroudsburg Cemetery. *#4116*

VIEWS OF THE COUNTY

You don't have to be a painter or photographer to appreciate Monroe County's splendor, although nature's wonders have lured artists and writers since the region was discovered. The Delaware Water Gap, alone, has been the subject of paintings displayed in New York and Philadelphia art galleries among others. Indeed one painting was by a Russian traveler in 1813 who used it as an illustration for a publication called "Picturesque Voyage in North America."

From the Gap, to the refreshing spectacles of Buck Hill Falls and Bushkill Falls to panoramic views available from Mount Pocono, the landscape offers a never-ending, ever-changing show. Even today's most densely built, commercial corridors are framed by picturesque mountain vistas.

These pages contain some views taken between 1836 and 1936 of towns and natural landmarks. Take the book with you on an afternoon exploratory mission to capture the same scenes today and compare the differences. Even the more built-up areas are beautiful.

Walk along Fulmer Street in Stroudsburg to see the view pictured on page 118 from Crowley's Heights. For a clearer view, you'll need to go when the trees are bare. Then head on down to Route 191, through South

The old dam, Analomink.

Stroudsburg, across Route 611 and up to where Stroudsmoor is now. That site used to be the Highland Dell House. From there, look north - if you can find a place to peek between homes and trees - and imagine how Stroudsburg looked in the 19th century.

A view of Analomink with Erich's Hotel in the foreground.

The end of Marshall's Walk, near Marshall's Creek. In 1739, Edward Marshall was one of the walkers in the infamous "Walking Purchase."

Buttermilk Falls, North Water Gap.

Marshalls Creek and Water Gap Falls.

"Ye Old Bridge" Marshall's Creek.

A view of Saylorsburg including Blue Ridge Brick Works.

A view of Stroudsburg.

A view of Stroudsburg as seen from Crowley's Heights, circa 1905.

A view of Stroudsburg from Highland Dell Road.

The upper Glen at Buck Hill Falls, circa 1914.

FEATURED BUSINESSES

The train station at East Stroudsburg, early 1900s.

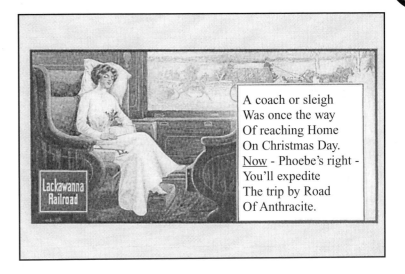

A coach or sleigh
Was once the way
Of reaching Home
On Christmas Day.
<u>Now</u> - Phoebe's right -
You'll expedite
The trip by Road
Of Anthracite.

ABOUT THE DEPOT *The Original 1864 Train Station*

The Dansbury Depot railroad station and freight house was built in 1864, in what was known then as the town of Dansbury. The station was beautifully landscaped with a fountain and colorful flower beds located on the East side of the station.

In 1900, Phoebe Snow was introduced in one of the finest early advertising campaigns ever launched. The catchy illustrated jingles featured Phoebe Snow displaying the beauty of her white gown, while riding on the train that used the clean-burning anthracite coal. Several of these ads are displayed in the Phoebe Snow Lounge at Dansbury Depot. During World War II, the Depot was used as a canteen for servicemen while the troop trains stopped for water. The Ladies' Auxiliary from the local V.F.W. served sandwiches, cake, cookies and coffee to more than 10,000 servicemen. During the heyday of the D.L.&W. passenger service, great crowds of people formed, at and around, the East Stroudsburg Depot, especially at the train time when many adults and youths came to the Pocono camps, resorts, and hotels at vacation time.

In 1949 a new passenger train was introduced as the most highly developed diesel train of that time. The train was renamed the "Phoebe Snow"; with its diesel and all new cars it would be fitting of the best traditions of cleanliness and modernity which the original Phoebe Snow has stood for. As time went on, railroad passenger service was replaced by automotive, truck, and bus service to the point that passenger trains were discontinued in 1970.

Today Conrail owns the old D.L.&W. Rail Line and has served the line by removing track from one of America's most featured rail lines ever.

PHONE 570-476-0500 or FAX 476-0541 – BE SURE TO VISIT OUR WEB SITE: www.dansburydepot.com

THERE'S NO PLACE LIKE HOME

1915-2000

Eighty-five years ago, Pocono Medical Center started with 15 beds, 13 employees, and the idea that people should not have to travel far to get superior medical care. As the region grew, the Medical Center, its staff, associated physicians, and services grew, too.

From those humble beginnings, Pocono Medical Center has continued to serve the needs of the community by providing the area with a cancer center; cardiology department; inpatient medical/surgical services; obstetric services; behavioral health services; outpatient services on-site as well as a freestanding center; and an emergency department that accommodated more than 51,000 patient visits last year.

From the people we employ, to the physicians we work with, to the services we offer, we're proud to say...

We bring superior care close to home.

POCONO
MEDICAL
CENTER

206 East Brown Street
East Stroudsburg, Pennsylvania 18301
(570) 421-4000

Business with a personal touch from J.L. Williams Jr. . . . . . .

J.L. Williams on Lower Main St. in Stroudsburg

"Business with a personal touch." For 73 years this has been the motto of the Williams family, who own and operate the J.L. Williams Jr. Appliance sales and service store located at 422 Main Street, Stroudsburg.

J.L. Williams Sr. started the family business in his front parlor in 1927 because of a need in the community for a quality appliance dealer and servicing center. The Williams family moved the business to its present location in 1946, after the need for expansion became evident with the business' strong following of clientele. The Williams family have continued to upgrade their store through remodeling over the years.

The third generation business founded by John L. Williams Sr. and his wife Martha is presently owned and operated by J.L. Williams Jr. and his wife Anna. Contributing to the thriving business is Gerrit Van Solkema Jr., the general manager and service technician along with his wife Ann Van Solkema (Williams' daughter) who works as a part time secretary and sales clerk for the business. And of course the future business leaders Gerrit III and Rachael (Williams' young grandchildren) frequently "help out" in the store.

J.L. Williams Jr. is the only authorized Hotpoint dealer in the Stroudsburg area. The Williams family attends courses and training seminars for sales and service, in order to keep up with technical advancements and to continue to provide their customers with quality service.

The Williams family prides themselves on providing quality sales and service in a friendly and courteous manner. J.L. Williams Jr. bases its sales on customer needs rather than concentrating on profit margins. Their aim as a family has always been "satisfied customers." This plus their continued improvement on sales and service provides them with the combination for a successful future.

J.L. Williams Jr. would like to extend a heartfelt thank you to all our customers from the past, the present, and in the future.

1927-1987 Father & Son Business

J.L. Williams went into the electrical contracting and house wiring business in Jan. 1927. In May of 1940 he was signed up as a Hotpoint Appliance dealer and in April 1946 moved to the present location, 422 Main St., Stroudsburg. Mr. J.L. Williams Sr. retired Dec. 1969, his son John Jr., who grew up in the business, took over and has had a very successful business since that time. Assisting him are his wife, Anna, son, John and son-in-law Gerrit.

J.L. Williams Sr. has come back to assist the family and now is semi retired. The family motto is "Business With A Personal Touch." Their aim has always been "Satisfied Customers", because of this they have been serving repeat customers for a proud 60 years.

1927
73 Years
2000
Authorized Sales & Service
Since 1927

J.L. WILLIAMS JR.
G.E. & Hotpoint Appliance Center
422 Main St., Stroudsburg
(570) 421-4910

Past
and
Present

Kresge-LeBar Drug Store
630 Main St., Stroudsburg, PA

Horse-drawn sleighs await in front of the LeBar's Drug Store, the only business in the 600 block of Main St. still in operation today from the 1800s. This photo was taken about 1906.

LeBar Rexall Drugs, 1950

Records show that as early as 1848 prescriptions were brought to this old apothecary shop, some from as far away as Newton, NJ. Founded by a member of the Hollinshead family, it was eventually purchased in 1880 by Dr. Amzi LeBar, a Stroudsburg physician. It quickly became known as LeBar's Drug Store, and for generations of local residents the tradition was, "Go to LeBar's Drug Store and get it."

The Kresge Drug Co. of East Stroudsburg was founded in 1917 by Harry Kresge, a local druggist. Subsequently owned by Park Unangst and then William and Marjorie Fizette, it was destroyed by the Crystal St. block fire in 1978. The Fizettes then purchased the LeBar Drug Store and combined the names, forming Kresge-LeBar Drug.

These two local names, Kresge and LeBar, representing over 200 years of pharmaceutical service to the community, are proudly displayed on the present marquis at 630 Main St., the site of the original Hollinshead store. The present store, managed by pharmacist and son Bob Fizette, is a combination of the latest technology for the dispensing of pharmaceuticals, combined with the traces of its history for all to see. In the midst of a busy dispensing practice, prescription compounding, almost a lost art in contemporary pharmacies, is practiced daily. The hallmark of the old community drug store, providing personalized service to each customer, continues.

The grand reopening after the 1950 renovation

Kresge-LeBar Drugs today

SUMMATION

We hope you've enjoyed exploring the images of the past as much as we did in compiling this book. It was a rewarding experience to work with the Monroe County Historical Association to bring our readers this unique look at Monroe County's heritage. It is evident that our history is steeped in diverse cultures and abundant natural resources.

Each photo reflects just how much the region has changed through the years. One constant throughout history is that change is inevitable. But the same qualities that attracted early pioneers continue to draw newcomers to the area. We are fortunate to enjoy scenic beauty, rich natural resources, and diverse opportunities.

As we begin the new millennium, we can look to the past for valuable insight. As we savor our rich history, we must be mindful that each of us is the caretaker of today, creating the images of Monroe County that will influence the quality of life for future generations.

Pocono Record

A reason to read... every day!